Nature Upclose

A Pill Bug's Life

Written and Illustrated by John Himmelman

Children's Press®
A Division of Scholastic Inc.
New York Toronto London Auckland
Sydney Mexico City New Delhi Hong Kong
Danbury, Connecticut

For Eddie Jeny, my childhood partner in "ballie" hunting

Library of Congress Cataloging-in-Publication Data

Himmelman, John.
    A pill bug's life / written and illustrated by John Himmelman.
       p. cm. — (Nature upclose)
    Summary: Describes the daily activities and life cycle of a
pill bug or wood louse.
    ISBN 0-516-21165 (lib. bdg.)   0-516-26798-1 (pbk.)
    1. Armadillidium vulgara—Life cycles Juvenile literature.
[Wood lice (Crustaceans)] I. Title. II. Series: Himmelman,
John. Nature upclose.
QL444.M34H56 1999
595.3'72—dc21   99-30137
                       CIP

**Visit Children's Press on the Internet at:
http://publishing.grolier.com**

GROLIER
PUBLISHING

© 1999 by Children's Press®
a Division of Grolier Publishing Co., Inc.
All rights reserved. Published simultaneously in Canada.
Printed in the United States of America.
    3 4 5 6 7 8 9 10 R 08 07 06 05 04 03 02 01

Pill Bug
Armadillidium vulgare

Large communities of pill bugs often live together in dark, damp places. They can be found under rocks and logs in wooded areas throughout North America. Pill bugs are full grown by their first fall and may live up to three years.

When a pill bug feels threatened, it rolls up into a tight ball. The hard outer covering on a pill bug's back protects it from enemies. Rolling up in a ball also keeps a pill bug's body moist.

A female pill bug has a large, well-hidden pouch running the length of her belly. She carries her eggs in the pouch. When pill bugs hatch, they stay in the pouch for several weeks. The little pill bugs crawl out when they are old enough to take care of themselves.

Pill bugs are not insects. They are closely related to lobsters, crabs, and shrimps. Many school classrooms keep pill bugs because they are easy to raise.

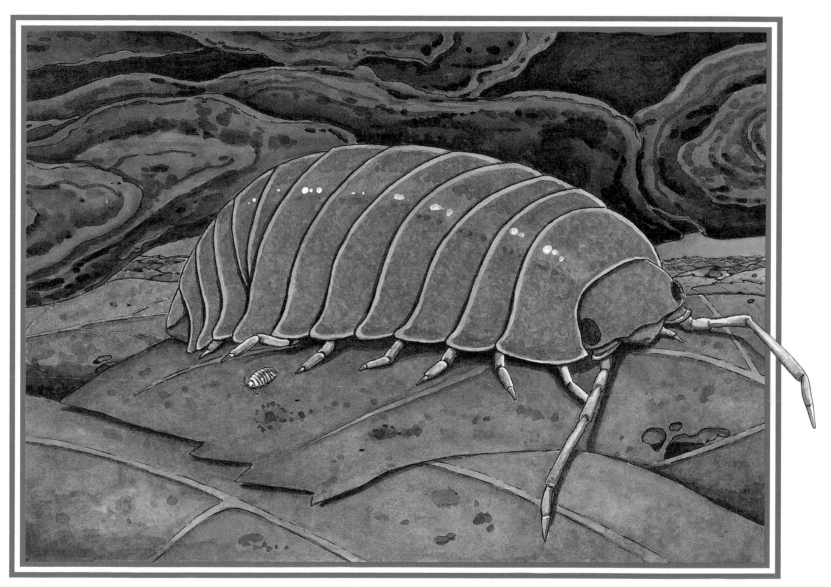

It is a spring morning. A young pill bug crawls out of a pouch on her mother's belly.

So do many other little pill bugs.

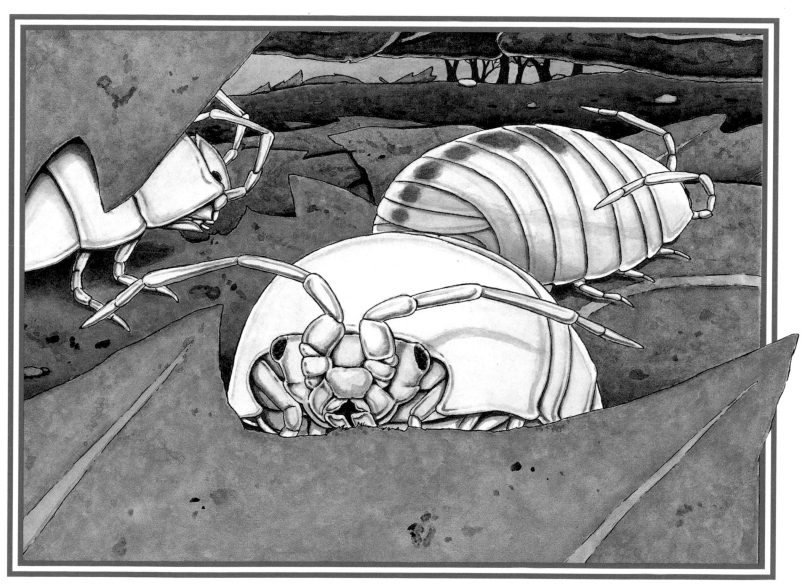

The pill bugs spend most of their time eating. They grow very fast.

Soon the pill bug is too big for her skin. She sheds the front half.

A few days later, she sheds the back half.

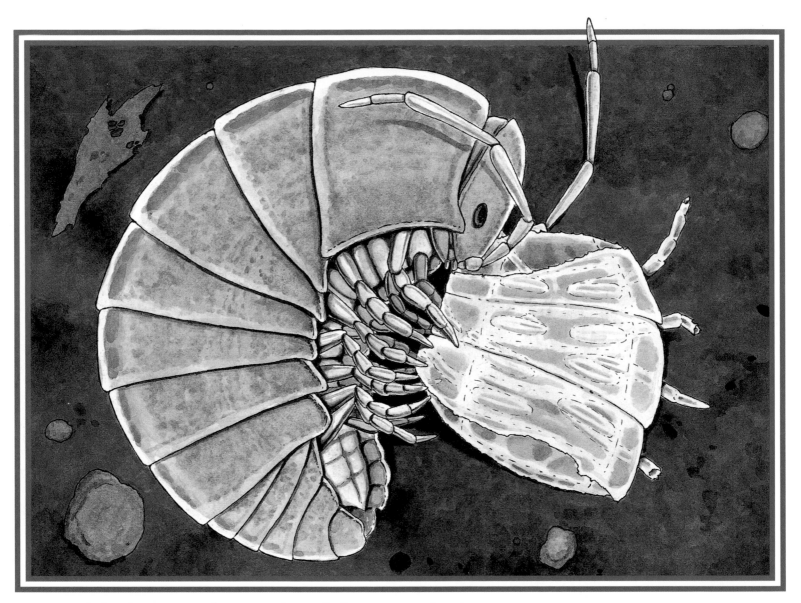

Her old skin makes a healthy meal.

All summer long, the pill bug changes and grows. When danger
comes near, . . .

. . . the pill bug rolls into a tight ball. The hungry *harvestman* moves on.

The pill bug crawls under a log. She is looking for dead leaves to eat.

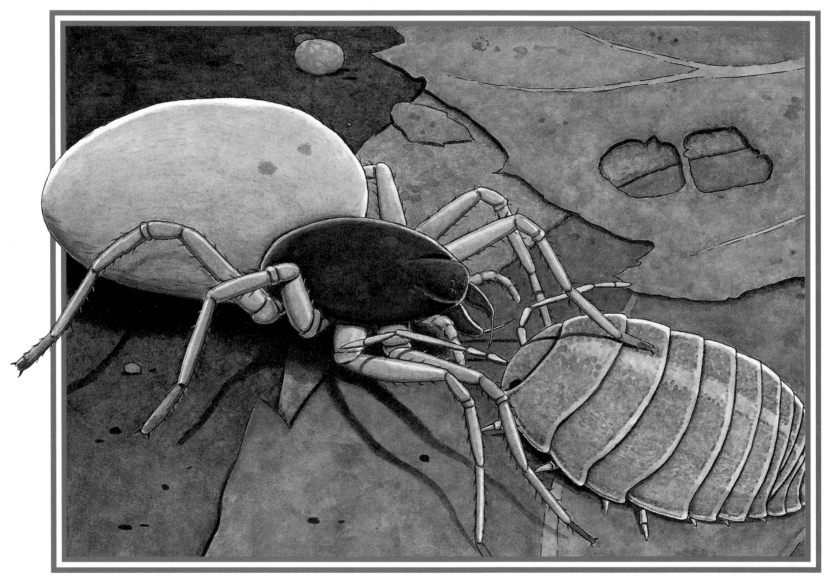

A *Dysdera spider* is under the log, too! It is looking for pill bugs to eat.

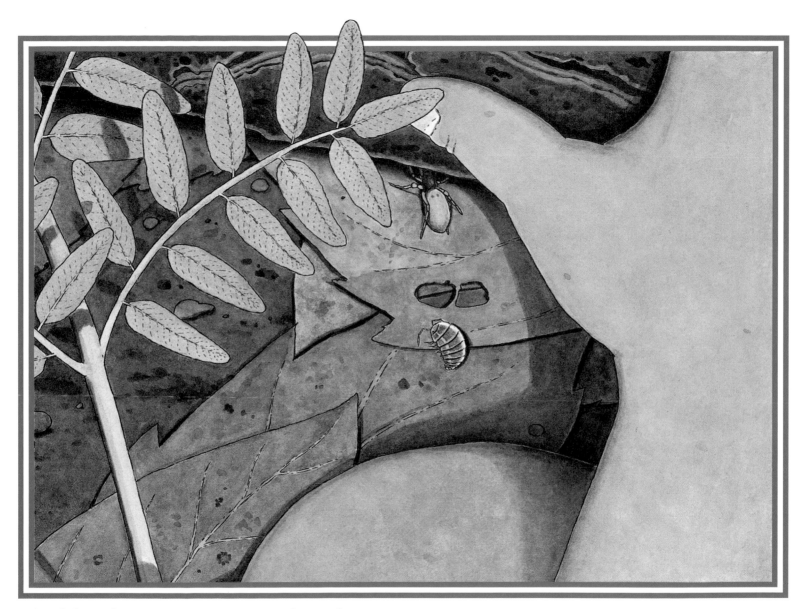

Suddenly, it gets very bright.

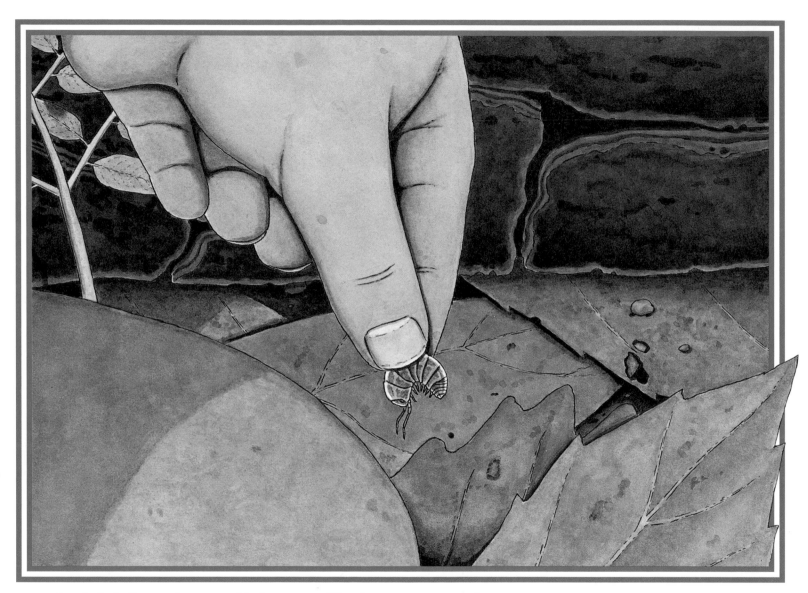

A child lifts the pill bug off the ground . . .

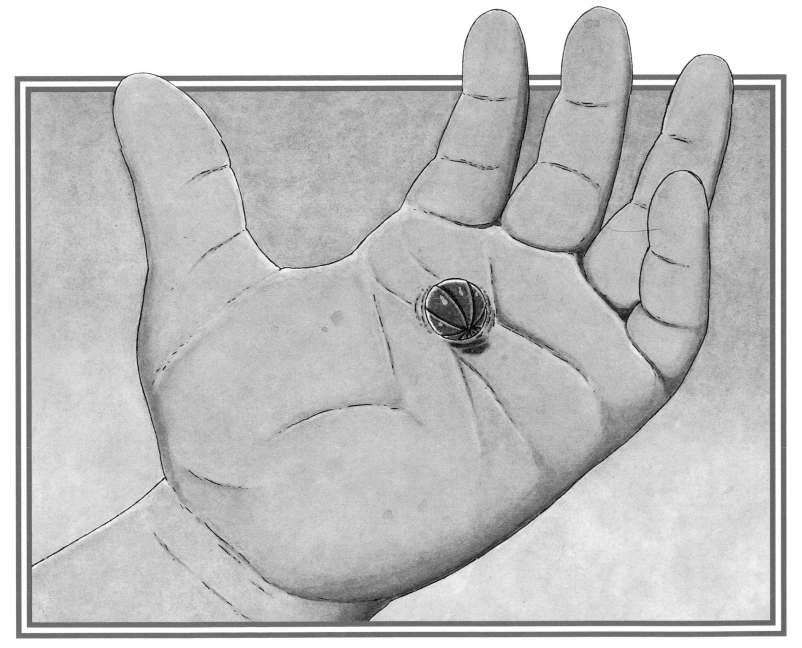

. . . and rolls her around and around.

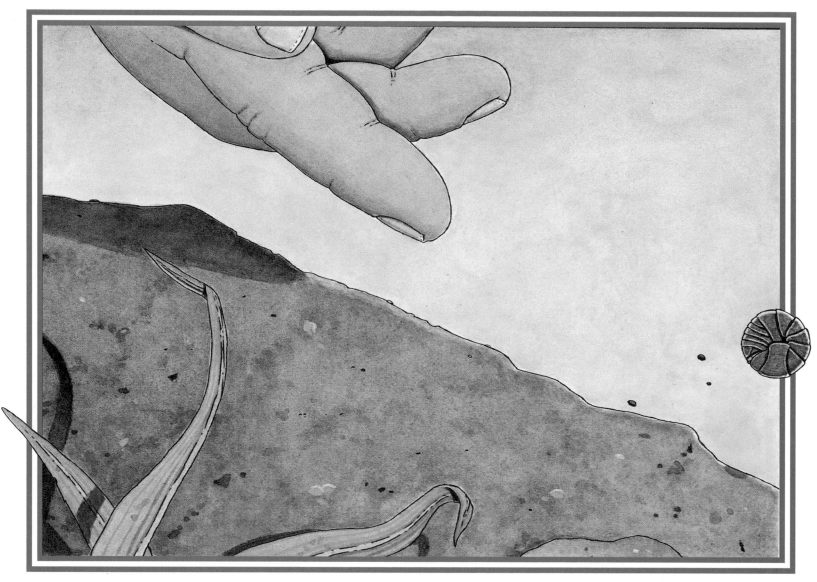

The pill bug rolls across a flat rock.

Finally, the danger has passed. The pill bug wanders through the forest.

She finds a large, dead log.

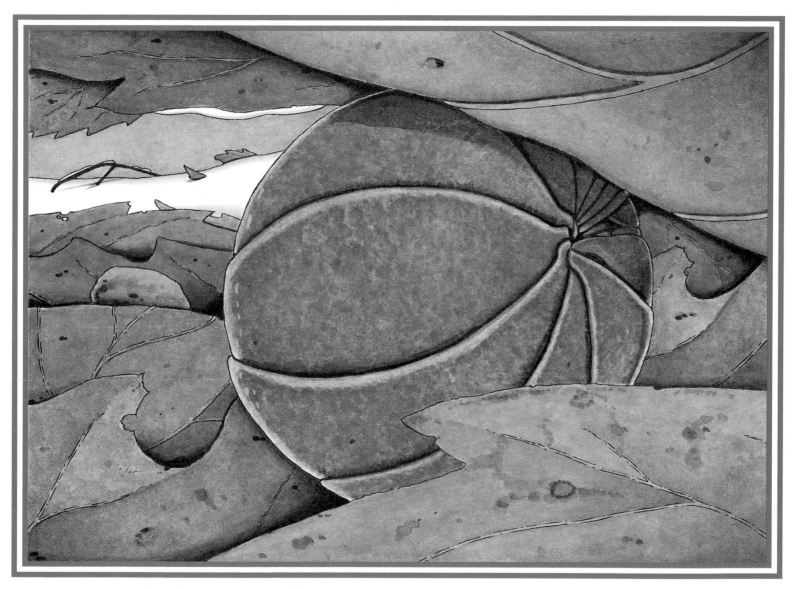

It is a good place to roll up and sleep through the winter.

Other pill bugs roll up, too. They do not want to dry out.

On warm winter days, the pill bug wakes up. *Snow fleas* wake up, too.

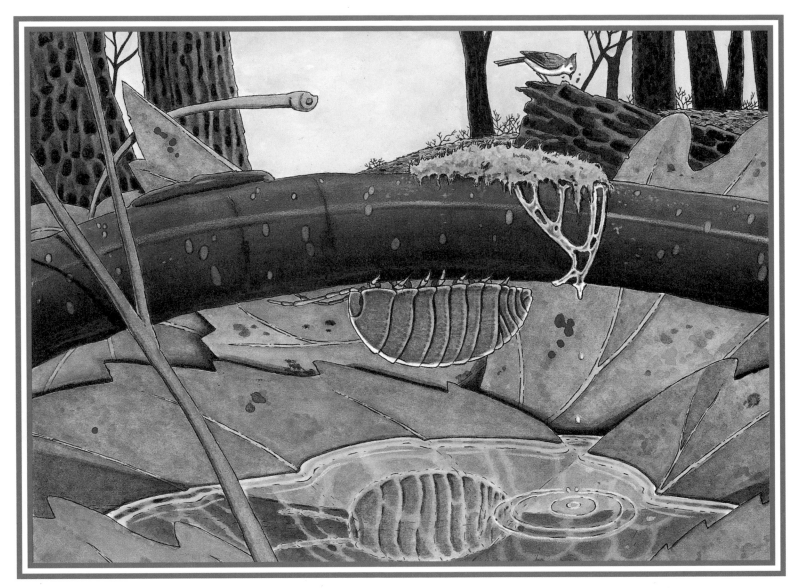

Soon the cool, damp spring comes. The pill bug wanders
across the forest floor.

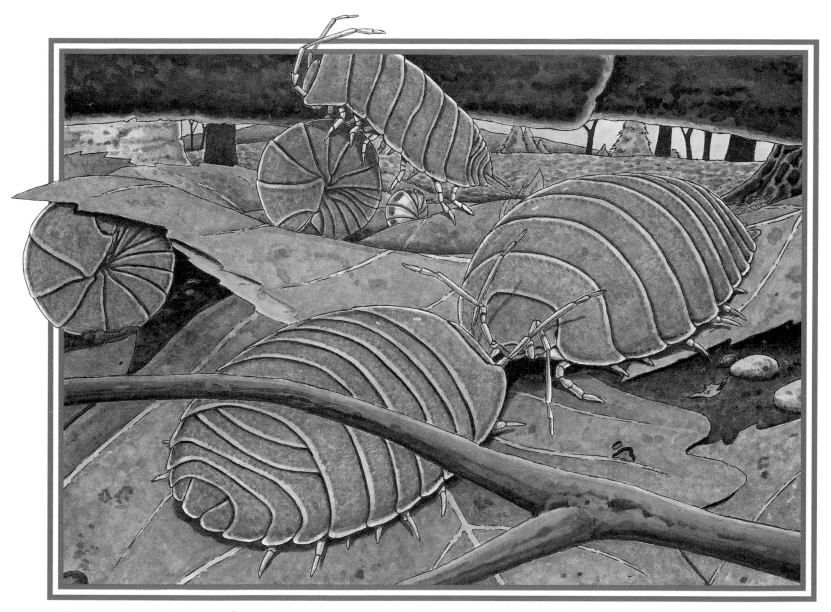

She is looking for a male pill bug. At last, she finds a mate.

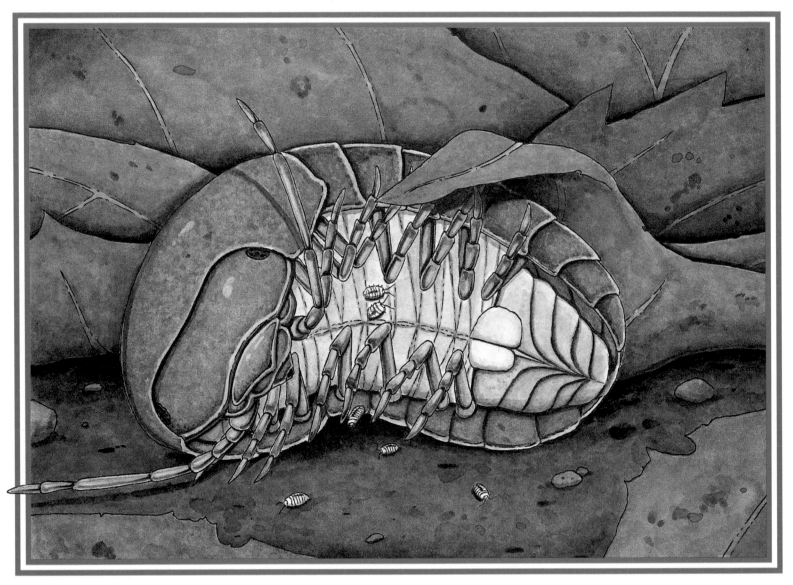

A month later, young pill bugs crawl out of the pouch on her belly.

They feed together under a log.

For the next three years, the pill bug hides out in cool, dark places.

She eats dead leaves . . .

. . . and has many close calls!

Each winter, she sleeps rolled up under a log.

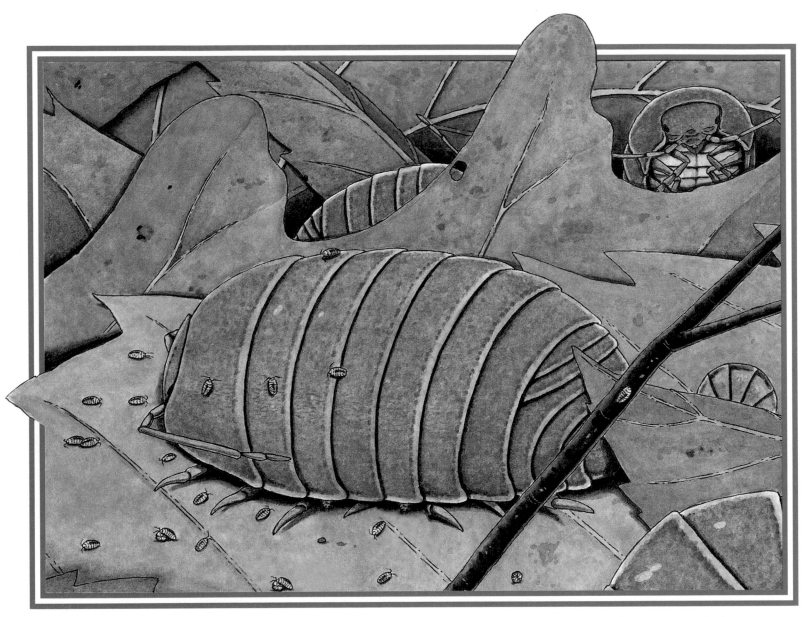

And every spring, she brings new pill bugs into the world.

Words You Know

harvestman—a long-legged cousin of spiders

Dysdera spider—a spider that lives under rocks and logs. Its main food is pill bugs.

snow fleas—tiny insects with springlike tails. They gather in large groups on warm winter days.

About the Author

John Himmelman has written or illustrated more than fifty books for children, including *Ibis: A True Whale Story, Wanted: Perfect Parents, The Animal Rescue Club,* and eight other books in the Nature Upclose series. His books have received honors such as Pick of the List, Book of the Month, JLG Selection, and the ABC Award. He is also a naturalist who enjoys turning over dead logs, crawling through grass, kneeling over puddles, and gazing at the sky. His greatest joy is sharing these experiences with others. John lives in Killingworth, Connecticut, with his wife, Betsy, who is an art teacher. They have two children, Jeff and Liz.